THE MURDER OF THE PERFECT PRISONER

Addiction, Family, and the Crime That Shook Missouri

JAMES KIRKPATRICK DAVIS

Genius
Book Publishing

Published by:
Genius Book Publishing
PO Box 250380
Milwaukee Wisconsin 53225 USA
GeniusBookPublishing.com

ISBN: 978-1-958727-85-0

251010 HQ

CONTENTS

For:
Winifred Lee Kirkpatrick Davis
&
John Plantz Davis II
&
Michael Carter Davis

NEW BLOOMFIELD, MISSOURI

A place of multiple murders

NEW BLOOMFIELD, MISSOURI, POPULATION 753, IS A small town in Callaway County, centrally located at the intersection of Old U.S. Highway 54 and Redwood Drive. It is near the central part of Missouri, north of Lake of the Ozarks—about twelve miles from Jefferson City, the state capital. The land around the town is generally flat, and the town can be seen from a great distance. At ninety-seven percent of the population, most are descended from various European stock—German, Irish, British, French, and Norwegian.

The average household income for a family of four in New Broomfield is approximately $63,000, above the national average. The town and surrounding areas feature plentiful employment opportunities, with white and blue-collar jobs in the office, sales, healthcare, and factories. Commuting times to work may vary from five minutes to forty-five minutes. New Bloomfield, for the last one hundred seventy or so years, has mainly existed free of violent crime.

It seems unlikely that anyone heard the two shotgun blasts fired sometime between December 23 and 24, 2006, in a home at 2029 County Line Road 372.

"A rare failing of the legal system itself,
It will dishonor our system of capital punishment."

Michael A. Wolff
Former Chief Justice, Supreme Court of Missouri

"During his seventeen years in prison facing capital punishment, he has not had a single infraction in prison."

Potosi prison staff

BRIAN JOSEPH DORSEY

"... Brian Dorsey formed a drinking habit
that did not stop until he turned himself in to
the police..."

Edward D. French, PH.D
Emeritus Professor of Pharmacology

MOST PEOPLE WHO HAD KNOWN BRIAN DORSEY described him simply as a caring person, loyal to family and friends, who would do almost anything for anyone—a very positive person. On the football field, he was described as a good kid, a hard worker, and respectful.

His father, Larry Dorsey, was often out of control; he was an alcoholic and verbally and physically abusive to Brian and his mother, creating, over several years, a generally dysfunctional upbringing for Brian Dorsey.

Brian Dorsey's life changed at 16, when binge drinking and cocaine addiction started and continued for the next thirty or so years, well into his early fifties. His teenage friend, Michael Horne, wrote, "Addiction took over his life." Binging cocaine led him to episodes of extreme paranoia and, at times, incredibly bizarre personality disorders and behavior patterns, such as talking nonsensically. Another friend at the time, Rodney Nilges, said, "Brian was suicidal when he was using cocaine."

"[Brian] Dorsey started binge drinking when he was in high school after growing up in a household that revolved around his father's alcoholism," according to an assessment of Dorsey's substance abuse by Dr. Edward French. "By age 19, Dorsey was 'self-medicating' with booze and cocaine, which would later be diagnosed as a major depressive disorder. Dorsey formed a daily drinking habit that did not stop until he turned himself in to the police for Bonnie's murder…"

Dorsey's addiction was clearly documented by age 22. He told one friend he could not stop his craving for cocaine.

By age 50, he had attempted suicide three times and been had admitted to a psychiatric facility for treatment in 2003 and 2005, and was placed on suicide watch both times.

A person who had known Brian Dorsey for years, Stephanie Sheely, recalled, "When Brian was on a binge, he would lock himself inside his apartment and become depressed and suicidal." Kevin Hiatte, who had worked with Dorsey, said Brian often borrowed money from family members but "was easy to get along with. He was not a

mean drunk, but it looked like he would never grow up."
Brian Dorsey's wife, Erica, said he "never physically abused
her, but he did emotionally abuse her at times." They were
rarely together during their marriage of less than six
months.

Rodricca Jefferson, another friend, remembered he and
Brian Dorsey had "hung out together," and they had "both
been kicked out of drug court" about two months before
the December 23, 2006, Bonnie homicides in New Bloomfield. Jefferson added that, on December 26, he noticed
Dorsey's picture on television and that he was "a person of
interest." Jefferson tried to call Dorsey, but the phone was
"out of service." The last time he had been in Dorsey's
apartment, Jefferson reportedly saw a "pipe" used to
smoke crack cocaine. At that time, Jefferson himself was
on probation for "distributing narcotics."

Tim Hanock, a long-time Dorsey drinking friend,
evidently had contact with Dorsey on December 22 or 23,
the night before or the night of the Bonnie homicides.
Hancock and Dorsey were "almost every other day
friends" for about the "last eight months." Hancock
confirmed Dorsey "snorted cocaine." He also said Dorsey
would turn to cocaine after drinking beer and whiskey; he
drank "heavily on the weekends." It was common for
Dorsey to become violent after drinking alcohol. Tim's
wife recalled a drinking episode on December 22, 2006,
when her husband and Dorsey had been drinking at a
neighborhood bar and were later asked to leave due to a
disturbance, and the police were called. One thing led to
another, and Tim left the bar without Dorsey. Dorsey, who
was immediately enraged, called and threatened Tim. Tim

and his wife were concerned to the point that they locked their doors that Friday night—something most people did not do in their small town—the night before the Bonnie murders.

BENJAMIN WADE BONNIE

BENJAMIN WADE BONNIE, A NATIVE OF CHARITON, Iowa, was born October 29, 1978. He graduated from Knoxville High School in Knoxville, Iowa, and earned a degree in Applied Science from Des Moines Area Community College. He was the son of Gregg and Marilyn Beaty Bonnie. As an avid outdoorsman, he was a proud Harley Davidson owner who enjoyed fishing, hunting, and camping. He had worked as an auto mechanic at Blackwell's Garage and at Custom Muffler, both in Jefferson City, and at Becket's Auto Services in Ashland. After their marriage in 2005, Ben and Sarah moved to their new home, set on a beautiful 10-acre site near New Bloomfield, Missouri, where they enjoyed entertaining and family gatherings. On the night of December 23, 2006, at 10:54 p.m., Ben Bonnie used his credit card to purchase $12.41 of gas at the New Bloomfield, Missouri, Phillips 66 station. His life would end three hours later.

SARAH ANN MOSIER BONNIE

AT AGE TWENTY-FIVE, SARAH ANN MOSIER BONNIE WAS remarkably attractive. A native of Jefferson City, Missouri, she and Ben Bonnie were married on June 11, 2005, in Tebbetts, Missouri. Sarah had graduated from Jefferson City High School, became a Certified Medical Assistant, and worked as an Emergency Medical Technician. Employment followed at the City of Fulton in the Utilities Department, then at McIntire's Florist in Fulton, and then at the Summit Villa Assisted Living in Holts Center. Mike and Diana Mosier, of Tibbets, were her parents, and Ben and Sarah were the parents of Jade Marie Bonnie. Her siblings included two sisters, Krista Shikles of New Broomfield and Traci Sheley of Holts Summit, and a brother, Michael Mosier, of Jefferson City. A close friend, Cristina Case, had worked with Sarah at the florist's shop. They remained in touch—she last heard from Sarah Bonnie on December 22, 2006, when she ordered flowers from a Walmart in Fulton for her father, Mike Mosier.

This was the last use of Sarah's credit card, December 22 at 8:30 a.m. Her last day on Earth would follow the next day.

DECEMBER 23, 2006

"Dorsey has a major drug problem; Sarah was trying to clean him and get him away from drugs."

Diana Lynn Mosier
Sarah Bonnie's mother

"You are going to have to decide between Brian and me!"

Benjamin Wade Bonnie

DIANA MOSIER REMEMBERED HER LAST CONTACT WITH her daughter, Sarah Bonnie. She had dropped off her granddaughter, Jade, at the Bonnies' house at about 9:30 p.m. on December 23, 2006. Sarah was baking gingerbread; everything seemed normal.

Missouri State Highway Patrol Trooper C. A. Winters later asked Diana Lynn Mosier if she knew who was at the Bonnie house that last night, December 23. She said, "Benjamin, Sarah, Jade Marie, Darin Carel, and... Brian Dorsey."

The trooper asked, "Who is Darin Carel?" Diana Lynn explained, "Darin was a close friend of Ben and Sarah."

Winters then asked if Sarah and Ben were engaged in drugs. She said, "No, but Sarah's cousin, Brian Dorsey, was involved in drugs. The night of the 23rd," she added, "Sarah and Ben had picked up Dorsey at his apartment in Jefferson City sometime around 7:30 p.m. or so, to bring him back to their house to spend the night before the Christmas party the next day on the 24th, also in Jefferson City. Dorsey had a major problem, and Sarah was trying to clean him up and get him away from drugs."

Brian Dorsey called Sarah Bonnie's sister, Traci, at about 4:30 p.m. on December 23. Traci started the conversation and said, "What's up?" Dorsey said he needed a favor; Traci asked, "What is the favor?" Dorsey said he owed some people money and needed the money right away. Traci had heard all of this before from Dorsey and refused to loan him any money in any amount. Dorsey persisted and said he needed $130; he had to find the money, and he needed it immediately. Then he ended the call.

Traci then called Sarah Bonnie to tell her that Brian wanted to borrow some money; Sarah said Dorsey had already called her and said the actual amount was $140. Traci then confirmed that Dorsey had not contacted Sarah's sister, Krista Shikles, but he also tried to contact another cousin, Kevin Hiatte, by contacting his sister, Pam Brauner, who had also tried to help him in the past; she had had enough of Brian and ended the call. Dorsey's other frantic calls to family and friends to search for money that afternoon were unsuccessful.

However, a few minutes later, Traci called Sarah again

and quickly learned that Sarah and Ben Bonnie were on their way to Dorsey's upstairs apartment at 1308 West McCarty in Jefferson City; two angry drug dealers, a white woman and a black man, were now at his apartment demanding past due drug money from Dorsey or else. After that call ended, Traci was worried about what might happen to Brian Dorsey and also to Ben and Sarah Bonnie in such a strange and possibly dangerous situation. She talked to her husband and said she felt she should go, particularly since it involved Ben and Sarah. Jon Sheley understood but wanted her to stay home since there might be trouble at Dorsey's apartment, and he knew that Dorsey was involved with drugs. Traci said she was very concerned and thought Dorsey might be desperate for help, and again, she said she was also worried about Ben and Sarah. Jon wasn't happy about it, but he finally agreed she should go. He stayed home with the kids, and she headed to Jefferson City.

Meanwhile, Darin Carel, the longtime friend of Ben and Sarah, was alerted to the situation by Ben, who said there were people at Dorsey's apartment, and they would not leave. There might be trouble; it was a tense situation. He said that he and Sarah would try to make them go, but they might need help getting those people out of Brian's apartment. Sarah had told Darin that Dorsey owed $60 or $160 for, she assumed, drugs that were probably long past due; she said she had talked to Dorsey earlier, and he was totally "spun out." She and Ben planned to have Brian stay with them that night of December 23 since his parents, Patty and Larry Dorsey, would not be in town until Sunday, December 25.

After arriving at the sidewalk below Dorsey's apartment in Jefferson City, Traci found Sarah and Darin standing outside. Sarah said a white woman standing before her did not want her to enter Dorsey's apartment, but Ben was allowed to go upstairs and into the apartment. Sarah assumed this was the same white woman who had been at Dorsey's apartment the day before at about two in the afternoon.

After entering Dorsey's apartment, Ben found Dorsey strung out high on crack/cocaine, sitting on his bed, waving his arms, and crying hysterically. Traci said this was common when Dorsey was strung out. The apartment itself was in complete shambles: clothes, trash, empty beer cans, whiskey, and vodka bottles were scattered everywhere on the floor; a pile of dirty laundry was in the bathroom; there was no toilet paper; vomit and human waste covered the bathroom floor.

After looking around at the chaos, Ben sat on the edge of the bed, rolled his eyes, and paid the woman $130. Then the two dealers quickly came out of the bedroom, apparently satisfied, and the black man asked if anyone had a beer or something like that. Darin got him a beer, and the couple left in a red Dakota pickup.

Ben had recently learned that Sarah had been giving money to her cousin Brian to pay his drug dealers. Ben was not happy about it, particularly after paying another dealer $130 that night. A few days before, he had said to Sarah, "You are going to have to decide between Brian and me!"

At this point, Darin, Traci, and Sarah went up the stairs to the apartment where Ben was trying to calm Brian down, telling him the dealers were gone, and they needed to leave immediately. Sarah wanted to get Brian out of there before something else happened; she told him to get some clothes together quickly, put them in a bag, and bring them to their house to spend the night in New Bloomfield, away from this horrible mess, confusion, and these scary drug people.

Brian was glad to get out of there. He was somehow able to get himself together well enough to grab clothes and put them in a bag, shut the apartment door, and lock it. He went down the apartment stairs and got in the Bonnies' car next to Ben and Sarah's four-year-old daughter, Jade Marie.

At that point, Ben, Sarah, Jade Marie, and Brian left Jefferson City together at about 7:45 p.m. Darin Carel followed them closely in his truck. They stopped at Leubberings in Holts Summit to buy beer. Once they arrived at Ben and Sarah's home in New Bloomfield, Sarah's sister Traci called and said she, Jon, and the kids were on their way to the Bonnies' house.

After arriving at the Bonnie's home, Ben, Brian, and Darin walked out to the garage behind the house to play, what they called, "some serious pool and drink much cold beer." Darin later recalled seeing Ben's 20-gauge shotgun lying on the pool table that evening, while they were in the garage. He remembered moving the weapon to another table and opening the breech to see if it was loaded, but it was not. Darin later said he did not know where the shotgun was finally placed while they played pool. He also saw a .22-gauge rifle leaning against a wall. Ben was planning to clean and repair it sometime after Christmas. After Jon and Traci Sheley arrived, Jon joined the group in the garage. Ben, drinking heavily, went to the house for about 30 minutes. Carel knew Ben was pretty drunk and thought he might pass out, but he returned to the garage with

Sarah. She soon returned to the house. During this time, Jade Marie came out to the garage for a few minutes and went back into the house.

After arriving at the house, Traci found Sarah preparing desserts for the next day's family party. They talked for a while, and Traci began cleaning the house for Sarah. She washed the kitchen, living room, and laundry but did not clean the bedroom, which she described as "messy."

Later that evening in the garage, Darin said they started wrestling around, but it was all fun and nothing serious. He later remembered leaving Ben and Sarah's house at about 10:30 p.m. that night, December 23. Ben had asked Darin to stay overnight because he was drunk, but Darin left anyway, drove straight home, and passed out on the couch. If Darin had remained at Ben and Sarah's house for another hour that night, the murders might not have happened at all—or he could have been a victim too. As it was, all hell was about to break loose!

HOMICIDE

"Dorsey had evidence of a genetically based dual diagnosis condition, including major depressive disorder, anxiety disorder, and cocaine and alcohol use disorder with cocaine withdrawal and alcohol intoxication."

Dr. John Matthew Fabian
PsyD JD.ABPP Forensic Psychiatrist

ON THE NIGHT OF DECEMBER 23, 2006, BRIAN DORSEY'S appearance was described by Sarah Bonnie's sister, Traci, as wearing blue jeans, a "Titlist" ball cap, white tennis shoes, braces on his lower teeth, and a full beard, standing about five feet, seven inches, 275 pounds, brown hair, and a tattoo of "Superman" on his right arm. Dorsey had not seen his wife Erica since early October 2006, after a married life of about thirty days.

That same evening of December 23, Sarah Bonnie

checked her voicemail at 10:32 p.m. Darin Carel later confirmed that Sarah and Ben were alive when he left the residence as late as sometime after 10:45 p.m. that evening.

Dorsey had not slept for two or three days. He was high on crack/cocaine, which had created horrifying paranoid delusions. He was desperate for money to pay several drug dealers and to buy more drugs. Years of drug abuse and prolonged mental illness had reached a climax, and in a state of confused and enraged hostility, he made his way back outside the house to the shed where they had all played pool earlier that evening, picked up Ben's 20-gauge shotgun, and returned to the house. He entered Ben and Sarah's bedroom and demanded $130 from his cousin, Sarah Bonnie. She said no, which resulted in a loud, hysterical argument.

Brian Dorsey murdered Ben and Sarah sometime between December 23, 2006, at 11:00 p.m. and December 24, at 3:18 a.m. He fired directly at Sarah Bonnie, causing massive damage to her lower jaw with separation of her brain stem from the spinal cord combined with extensive cerebral edema. She died instantly. Dorsey quickly reloaded, fired, and hit Ben just under his left ear, shattering the midline and fracturing the left temporal bone. He died instantly as well. Then, Dorsey apparently made a fruitless attempt to hide evidence with Clorox.

Jade Bonnie, then four, evidently did not hear the two shotgun blasts. Before she fell asleep, Dorsey had locked the bedroom doors. Dorsey, known to her as "Beeg," told her to be still and stop "splaining" and talking or he said he would not lay down with her on the living room sofa. Jade remembered that Dorsey was on his knees when talking to her. She recalled that Beeg had on jeans, a "stripy" shirt, and a cap on backward.

Callaway County Sheriff Clay Chism was a deputy when Brian Dorsey committed both murders. "The scene was horrific," he recalled. "To this day, eighteen years later, I remember it like it happened yesterday. I just can't imagine the trauma the little girl suffered. That was a trauma that will never go away."

After the murders, Jade began talking about hearing someone sneaking in and killing her mom and dad, but she had no concept of the finality of death. She saw her grandparents crying and saw her dad with blood on his shoulder and her mother with one of her mom's legs touching the floor and the other on the bed, with blood on her legs too.

About the events leading up to December 23, 2006, Brian Dorsey later said his depression had been the worst he had ever experienced. He said he had hit a lot of rock bottoms in the past, but this one felt like a hole he could not get out of. There had been negative events in his life, including marriage failure, being arrested and charged for a hit-and-run while driving under the influence, his subsequent inability to conform to the requirements of the drug court when he wanted help with his addiction, and his chaotic living situation, far from family or good influences and unable to reach out for help easily because he did not have a car.

Dorsey can recall the events leading up to a point. He remembered that in the evening people who had provided him with drugs were now in his Jefferson City apartment demanding payment. He was deeply embarrassed when his family had to get involved. He recalled Sarah, Ben, Traci, and Darin coming to his apartment, and after Ben paid the drug dealers, going back with them to Ben and Sarah's house. He remembered playing pool in the garage behind the house and Sarah's daughter Jade coming into the garage and playing with a pool stick. He noticed Ben Bonnie's 20-gauge shotgun on the pool table, which he removed and opened the breech to see if it was loaded, which it was not. He did not remember where he put the shotgun after moving it from the pool table. He also recalled a .22 rifle in the garage that Ben Bonnie was repairing.

He remembered that when Traci and Jon Sheley arrived at the house, Jon went to the garage and joined Ben and the others. At one point, Sarah came out to the garage, talked to her husband, then returned to the house. Ben, Darin, Jon, and Brian did some pushing and shoving each other in fun and drank more beer. Ben, by this time, was drunk. Jon, Traci, and their kids left at about 9:45 p.m.

Dorsey remembered staying in the house after Darin and the others left. He recalled Ben and Sarah going to bed. He planned to sleep on the couch in the living room. He started watching TV and drinking beer. When he finished the beer, he started drinking whiskey straight from the bottle. He recalled going back to the garage where they had been playing pool earlier, seeing the gun there, and thinking about killing himself. That is the last thing he remembered from that night. His next memory is of the following day, December 24, 2006, and being with other people smoking crack. He thought something was wrong. He knew he had Sarah's car and saw the gun in the car. He called his mother and discussed killing himself. Then he slept for the first time in several days. When he woke up, after deciding he was not going to kill himself, he called his mother and asked her to pick him up.

The day before that call to his mother and immediately after killing Ben and Sarah he pillaged the Bonnie household of nearly a hundred household items including a 19' television, a DVD player, two cell phones and their chargers, Sarah Bonnie's Social Security card and driver's license, Sarah's Pontiac Grand Prix, jewelry, including diamond rings, a necklace, and earrings, four credit cards belonging to Ben and Sarah, a soft case for a Ruger MTI Bolt Action Rifle with a scope, and the murder weapon, a 20-gauge shotgun.

Phone records confirm that Brian Dorsey was still at the Bonnie residence after the murders at 3:36 a.m. on December 24. Dorsey was at his Jefferson City apartment by 3:56 a.m., twenty minutes later.

Detective Jeff Nichols, in testifying about the crime scene, said there was a strong odor of bleach in the bedroom, particularly near the bathroom and on the side of the bed where Sarah Bonnie was found. Detective Nichols also saw a bottle of bleach in the main bathroom and a discolored bleached-out carpet next to the bed where Sarah was lying. He saw what appeared to be a pour pattern. He used an alternative light source to enhance or look for fluids and determined that liquid had been poured in Sarah's groin area. A sexual assault kit was used to collect evidence from Sarah's body and the vaginal swabs taken were sent to the Missouri State Highway Patrol Crime lab for testing. A full profile was created from the swab indicating she was the source of the DNA swab, and later tests confirmed the profiles matched Dorsey as the source of the autosomal DNA.

Well before these crime scene tests were completed, Dorsey had stolen Sarah Bonnie's cell phone. He used it to make 10 calls between 3:59 a.m. and 6:18 a.m. He next made 40 calls also on Sarah's cell between 7:27 a.m. and 10:53 a.m.—almost certainly looking for money and drugs. On December 24, at 4:00 a.m., Patricia A. Cannella, a local drug dealer, reported Dorsey was trying to sell items stolen from the Bonnie residence. He was driving Sarah Bonnie's stolen car. He owed Cannella $180.

Laster in the day of December 24, Sergeant Bob Smith and Chief Deputy Darryl Maylee contacted Patty and Larry Dorsey at the Super 8 Motel in Jefferson City, room #222. They had heard from Brian late the night before on December 23. At that time, Brian was frenzied, nearly out of control, and desperate for $150 to pay drug dealers demanding money. Patty had heard Brian's drug hysteria before. She was blunt. She was not going to give him $150 to pay his unknown assortment of drug dealers, whoever or wherever they were. Then Brian demanded phone numbers for relatives to contact for money. Patty again said no, it would not happen. Brian hung up. Brian then planned to ask his cousin, Sarah Bonnie, for the money. He was desperate and she was his last hope.

They confirmed Brian had a major drug problem that began when he was a teenager. They released Brian's cell phone number to the police and confirmed he did not have a key to his parents' trailer home in Warsaw, Missouri.

The next day, December 25, Sergeant Bob Smith again contacted Patty Dorsey and asked if she had heard from Brian. She said she had not heard from Brian and was worried about his safety. Smith confirmed the sheriff's department was searching for him. Sergeant Smith recommended they call the Jefferson City Police Department for assistance. After that call, Patty contacted Smith again, and confirmed that the Jefferson City Police had listed Brian Dorsey as a missing person. Bob Smith then received a call from Jefferson City Police Sergeant Mathrum, who advised they had searched Brian's apartment in Jefferson City, where they discovered a pill bottle in the apartment with the name Julie Eakins on it. They started searching for her as a lead to finding Dorsey.

The following day, December 26, Brian, Patty, and Larry Dorsey arrived at the Callaway County Sheriff's Office and met with Chief Deputy Darryl Maylee, Officer Bill Akers, and Sergeant Bob Smith. They reported that, on December 26, at about 12:15 a.m. and again at 2:40 a.m., Brian Dorsey called his mother, Patty Dorsey, using Sarah Bonnie's cell phone and talked of suicide, but said he was too frightened to kill himself. He said he would call back and ended the call. He called his mother immediately after that, still using Sarah's cell, and asked his parents to pick him up. Patty and Larry Dorsey drove the thirteen miles to Jefferson City with the understanding that, once they were in the city, Brian would call with further directions. Patty and Larry found Brian standing next to Sarah Bonnie's Pontiac Grand Prix off Old Highway 94, close to Cedar City, Missouri.

Later on December 26, Sarah's car was searched, and police found the 20-gauge shotgun, a deer rifle, Ben and Sarah's cellphones, a camera, and jewelry. The headlights and taillights on Sarah's car had been disabled so Dorsey could run the engine without lights.

Meanwhile, Brian, Patty, and Larry Dorsey drove to

Kingdom City, Missouri, picked up snack food, and checked into room #109 at the Days Inn at 3:40 p.m. on December 26. At about 11:45 p.m. that night, Fulton Police Department Lieutenant Rich McKee and Missouri State Highway Patrol Sergeant Kurt Mueller contacted Jack Patel, the Days Inn owner, who confirmed that Brian, Patty, and Larry Dorsey left room #109 at about 10:00 p.m. that night. Room #109 was then searched. One pair of gray men's underwear and white socks were seized as evidence and turned into the Callaway County Sheriff's Office by Lieutenant Tim Osborne.

Brian had said he wanted to spend some time with his parents. He assumed it would be the last time he would be with them for a while. He took a shower and put on the same clothes he wore the day before when his parents picked him up next to Sarah's Pontiac at Old Highway 94. Brian could not talk about what had happened. When asked, he broke down violently, sobbing—it all seemed like a horrifying bad dream. He said Ben and Sarah Bonnie were his perfect friends. He thought highly of them and their daughter Jade.

At about 11:00 a.m. on December 26, 2006, Bob Smith was told by the Calloway County Sheriff's Office receptionist that a person named Brian Dorsey was in the lobby. Smith recognized Dorsey from his photo. He also recognized Patty and Larry Dorsey. They gathered in the front office interview room. Smith contacted the Major Case Squad and advised them that Brian Dorsey had turned himself in. His parents were sent to a separate interview room—interviews for all three were conducted by Sergeant Bob Smith, Sergeant Bill Akers, Chief Deputy

Darryl Maylee, and Missouri State Highway Patrol Investigator Rick Hendon.

During the interviews, according to his parents, it was said that it was Brian's idea to go to the Calloway County Sheriff's Office. Brian was taken to the same interview room as his parents, and spent about 15 minutes with them before they were separated. Patty and Larry Dorsey knew their son was in serious trouble related to the deaths of Brian and Sarah Bonnie. Dorsey said he wanted a public defender; his mother asked for advice. Chief Deputy Maylee gave her the number for the Missouri Bar Association. In the meantime, Brian had also told his parents he wanted to make things right and deserved whatever the courts would decide for his punishment. He signed a Waiver of Rights and Consent to Search form, consented to a buccal swab, and confirmed he knew his Miranda Rights.

Dorsey was instructed to remove his size #10 red/white Reebok tennis shoes, which appeared to be an exact match to the shoe prints left at the crime scene. Chief Investigator Tim Osborn secured the evidence.

Near the end of the first interview, Sergeant Bob Smith asked Dorsey three questions:

Sergeant Smith: You did not go to the Bonnies' house with the intention of hurting them, did you?

Dorsey: No, I did not.

Sergeant Smith: You did not plan or plot to go to the Bonnies and do that to them, did you?

Dorsey: No, I did not.

Sergeant Smith: Are we talking to the right man concerning the death of the Bonnies?

Dorsey: Yes.

Dorsey then said he did not wish to talk anymore until he talked with an attorney.

Chief Deputy Maylee secured inmate clothing to fit Dorsey and put his other clothing in an evidence bag. Maylee told Dorsey he was under arrest for two counts of murder in the first degree. Dorsey was taken to a cell and placed on suicide watch.

DECEMBER 24, 2006

"Oh my God!"

Mike Mosier
Sarah Bonnie's father

THE DAY BEFORE CHRISTMAS, SATURDAY, DECEMBER 24, 2006, Mike and Diana Lynn Mosier, Sarah Bonnie's parents, were at a holiday party at Sarah's parents' (Greg and Marie Bonnie's) home in Jefferson City, the family event of the year. All looked forward to seeing Sarah Ann Mosier Bonnie, son-in-law Benjamin Wade Bonnie, and four-year-old granddaughter Jade. All three were expected but did not arrive. Sarah's parents phoned Ben and Sarah's home at 12:15 p.m., 12:45 p.m., and then again at 1:00 p.m. There was no answer. Something *had to be* wrong. Another hour passed and still another, with more phone calls. Nothing. Why on this day, of all days, did they not answer? Finally, at almost 3:00 p.m., Mike and Diana decided to find out what was happening. They arrived at 2029 County Line Road in New Bloomfield at 3:15 p.m. that afternoon.

When they stopped in front of Ben and Sarah's house, Sarah Bonnie's white 1997 Pontiac Grand Prix was not in front of the house, in the two-car detached garage, in the driveway, or in the barn. Was Sarah in the missing car? Where was Ben? Where was Jade? They saw an older pickup truck in the front yard, a small passenger car next to the detached garage, and a maroon sports car behind the small passenger car.

Although Sarah's car was missing, everything else seemed normal; nothing looked out of place. Mike and Diana made their way up the sidewalk to the front of the modular home—a double-wide trailer with a detached garage. Mike was leading—it was a quiet day with a deep blue sky, not a breeze, not a sound anywhere. The front interior door to the residence was closed, and an exterior screen door was open. Mike looked through the screen door; a television set was in operation, and his grand-daughter, Jade, was sitting on a living room couch. Mike and Diana Lynn went in. Jade, glad to see her grandfather and grandmother, smiled and said, "Mommy is still sleeping." Diana Lynn picked her up. Mike assumed Sarah and Ben were still in the bedroom so he knocked on the main bedroom door at the north end of the house. No response. He turned the doorknob. The door was locked. Mike and Diana looked at each other then walked through the kitchen to the other bedroom door. It was also closed. Mike found a screwdriver below the kitchen sink and opened the kitchen bedroom door by slowly forcing it open. He took a few steps into the bedroom and called for Sarah and Ben—not a sound. Then:

"Oh my God!"

There was blood on the bed. Sarah Bonnie was on the bed, covered partially by a blanket with blood smeared on her face. Ben was slumped over on the bed next to Sarah. Mike saw a bloody hole on the right side of Ben's face, just under his right ear. He checked for Sarah's pulse; there was none. She was cold to the touch. He realized Ben was dead too. Diana later remembered screaming, which terrified Jade, who started crying hysterically. Mike, horrified, his face covered with tears, wiped his face, turned, and told his wife to keep hold of Jade and get out of the house. He retraced his steps, left the house, made it back to the driveway, told his wife he was going back into the house, and told her to get in their Ford truck with Jade. She called 911. He went back into the house and up and down the hallways, searching every room. He found no one else in the house.

The response was immediate. Calloway County Sheriff's officers Lance Roberts, Bob Smith, Chief Deputy Darryl Maylee, Dennis Crane, Kirk Biehm, and Missouri State Highway Patrol Trooper Chris Winters were the first to arrive at the Bonnie house crime scene. Sergeant Clay Chism was designated as the primary evidence collector and eventually took custody of all the evidence collected, assisted by Collector Sergeant Shannon Jefferies.

Officers Roberts and Biehm and Trooper Winters approached the house for a preliminary search. As they entered the house, they noticed the television in the living room was on. They turned it off and made their way to the north bedroom and pushed the door open. They saw a blood spot on the bedroom carpet, and that both victims, covered with blood, were deceased. They searched the rest of the house. A small black cocker spaniel, found sitting on a living room couch, was taken outside.

At about 3:36 p.m., Trooper Winters and sheriff's officers left the house and noticed a blue Chevy pickup in the yard that they would soon find belonged to Brian Dorsey, as well as a gray Ford Pickup in the driveway. On the edge of hysteria, Diana Mosier was now standing outside on the driveway next to the Ford pickup, holding her granddaughter.

CHIEF DEPUTY DARRYL MAYLEE

"I then noticed the body of Sarah Bonnie lying on the right side of the bed."

Chief Darryl Maylee,
Callaway County Sheriff's Department

AT ABOUT 3:45 P.M., CHIEF DEPUTY MAYLEE ENTERED the house and "found the living room in disarray; a child's board game and other toys and dog feces were on the floor." He added, "Between the sofa and coffee table in the living room, I saw areas of blood and partial footprints on the floor leading to the main bedroom, which was in shambles. Clothing and other items were scattered on the bed and floor. On the main bedroom floor, in front of the main floor area in front of the bed, I noticed an empty knife sheath. I then noticed the body of Sarah Bonnie lying on the right side of the bed. She was wearing a blood-covered T-shirt lying on her back, partially covered with bed covers; her left leg was hanging off the bed; there was what looked like a bloody 'swipe' across the bottom part of her leg; her right leg looked partially pulled up to her stomach. On the floor, on the right side of the bed, I saw what appeared to be bleach burns on the carpet. Ben Bonnie was on the left side of the bed; he was wearing boxer shorts; his knees were on the floor with the upper part of him on the bed; his arms were folded. I did not touch the victims; I did not see firearms and left the residence."

One spent 20-gauge shell was found in the kitchen sink. Blood spatters were found on Christmas presents in the living room and on a wastebasket containing a sleeping bag near the entrance to the main bedroom. Spatter was also found on a Victoria's Secret box behind a closed door in the entertainment center. Blood was found on carpeting in many parts of the house—possibly spread by the dog left overnight in the house. Later police found cell phones and a jewelry box were missing along with a Titlist ball cap, a fleece dark blue jacket, a gray New York Yankees T-shirt, a gray Missouri Tigers T-shirt, a blood-stained bedsheet pillowcase, a Paris Road Pawnshop ticket regarding the sale of a Ruger 308 rifle to Ben Bonnie in October 2001, a bottle of sweet and sour mixer from the kitchen, and a bleach container. Latent prints were found on the switch within the far south bedroom and on the lid of another Victoria's Secret box.

An hour later, at about 4:51 p.m., a dark four-door passenger car with two passengers was allowed past the County Road 372 roadblock and stopped in front of the now cordoned-off 2029 County Road modular home. Ben Bonnie's father, Greg Bonnie, was in the car and was told to remain in his vehicle. A few minutes later, Officer Roberts and Greg Bonnie then walked a distance away from the back of the vehicle, and Roberts quietly told Ben Bonnie's father that his son had passed away. Greg Bonnie, shattered and stunned, broke down and asked how his son had died. Roberts told him that at this point in an ongoing investigation, he could not give him that information. A few minutes later, Greg Bonnie, distraught, said he would have to leave soon to tell his wife, Marilyn Bonnie, in person what had happened. Greg Bonnie then asked to see Mike Mosier, Sarah's father. They cried together with their arms around each other.

Lieutenant Tim Osburn, with Officers Chism and Jefferies, searched the main bedroom crime scene after contacting Dori Burk at the Boone and Callaway County Medical Examiner's office.

Once inside the main bedroom, he saw the two victims, Ben and Sarah Bonnie, both dead on the bed. Both had noticeable head wounds. Osburn collected a GSR (gunshot residue) kit from the hands of both victims. This was done to determine if either one might have held a discharged firearm. The results were negative. Next, using an alternative light source (ALS), Osburn examined both victims for any evidence not visible to the naked eye. He did notice some kind of fluid on Sarah's groin, upper legs, and waist. He then noticed bleached carpeted areas where the fluid had run off Sarah's left leg down to the carpeted floor. This seemed to explain the pungent odor of bleach in the bedroom. The stained carpeted area near the bed was cut out and removed, and a bleach container was found in the adjacent bedroom. A swab from the upper portion of Sarah's left leg would be collected again during the autopsy using ALS system technology.

Next, on both the bedroom and living room floors, Osburn saw what appeared to be areas of blood spatter, consistent with impact spatter and blood transfer. Then, using Luminal to detect blood evidence not visible to the naked eye, he screened every room in the house as well as the hallways. There were visible transfer stains consistent with dog paw prints. On the bedroom wall, behind the headboard, was an area consisting of tissue fragments, blood stains, and shot impact patterns. A lead shot was found on the floor and would be found to be consistent with the lead shot recovered from the victims during the autopsy. Finger and palm prints of the victims were taken. Officers at the scene also found a shotgun wad, three empty Budweiser bottles, a smoked cigarette, a pack of cigarettes, bloody blue jeans, female underwear, a Pepsi can, and a shotgun on the floor close to Ben Bonnie, as well as the contents of his wallet, and some of the items from Sarah's purse.

Officers next reported that Ben Bonnie should have a 308 rifle, a 20-gauge shotgun, and a dismantled .22. rifle in the shed behind the house. When they looked, they found an empty gun case on the barbecue grill outside the shed door. They noted that a dark-colored pickup was parked in the front yard. The driver's side door was open, and the vehicle was filled with trash, along with a tremendous amount of trash on the ground under both doors. Also under the driver's side door was a muddy shoeprint, later confirmed to have been placed there by shoes similar to the tennis shoes Brian Dorsey was wearing at the time of his arrest.

It was not long before ambulances arrived, along with the coroner, a police photographer, state troopers, more police officers, and people from the radio and newspapers. Many family members and friends of the Bonnie and Mosier families, and strangers primarily from Callaway and surrounding counties, were also on scene but none were allowed past the police barricade, which was briefly lifted to permit the exit of two ambulances.

Both victims were removed from the house at 9:16 p.m. and taken to the medical examiner's office. The residence, shed, and vehicles were sealed by Sergeant Chism at about 10:15 p.m.

An autopsy was scheduled for December 26 at 10:30 a.m.

TRIAL: A FLAT-FEE DEFENSE DISASTER

" No one in their right mind would take a flat fee for a capital case; no ethical attorney would even consider it."

Cheryl Pilate
Attorney
Kansas City

"I think the idea was that we were hoping for some credit or acceptance of responsibility from the jury."

Christopher A. Slusher

THE MISSOURI PUBLIC DEFENDER'S OFFICE APPOINTED Cristopher A. Slusher and Scott T. McBride to represent Brian Dorsey, regardless of whether or not the case would go to trial. They would each be paid a flat fee of $12,000, which would amount at the time to less than one-fifth of the payment per hour established by the Federal Judiciary for defense attorneys working in capital/death penalty cases. Flat fee representation fails to provide the level of representation stipulated by the Sixth Amendment and the Due Process Clause. Flat fee representation is now prohibited in most states.

One analysis reveals that between 1998 and 2004, defense lawyers generally spent about 3,600 hours working on capital/death penalty cases per trial. As noted, Slusher and McBride were paid $24,000. If they had devoted 3,600 hours to defend Brian Dorsey, they would have been paid about $6.70 per hour. Kansas City defense attorney Cheryl Pilate, who has handled dozens of capital/death penalty cases, said, "Those cases take thousands of hours of hard work. They are long, exhausting, and unpredictable. No one in their right mind would take a flat fee for a capital case because it puts you in direct conflict with the client. No ethical attorney would even consider it."

On March 10, 2008, fourteen months after the December 23-24, 2006, multiple murders in New Bloomfield, Missouri, Dorsey appeared in Boone County Circuit Court to begin the scheduled evidentiary hearing, which followed the penalty phase / jury trial.

Jurors had been selected two years earlier, and a sentencing hearing officially began several months earlier. Circuit Judge Gene Hamilton would ultimately decide the sentence, but the sentence could not exceed the jury's recommendations.

On March 9, 2008, the day before Dorsey's evidentiary hearing and sentencing trial began, Christoper A. Slusher called Janet Thompson, an appellate lawyer in the state public defender's office. Slusher said he planned to have Dorsey plead guilty even though there was no arrangement with the prosecutors to take the death penalty out of consideration. Ms. Thompson later wrote, "I told him it was a really bad idea; every time that anybody had done that kind of procedure, the result had been abominable."

Janet Thompson later testified at a 2011 post-conviction hearing that the idea of pleading guilty was given to Brian Dorsey on the morning of his plea hearing, with virtually no time for Dorsey to consult with his parents or anyone about this critical life-and-death decision. She had reported her concerns to her supervisor at the time. ABA guidelines advise lawyers in death penalty cases to be "extremely reluctant" to waive a client's trial rights without a guarantee that the death penalty will not be imposed. Slusher and McBride made a disastrous life-and-death decision on March 10, 2008; it would cost Brian Dorsey his life. Ms. Thompson later wrote, "I further opined that the system should not hire Mr. Slusher or Mr. McBride for a death penalty case again."

Slusher and McBride, by their own admission, did virtually no investigation whatever, did not work with investigators, whom the public defender's office would have paid, and instead recommended that their client, Brian Dorsey, plead guilty to first-degree murder the day before the evidentiary hearing began.

They convinced Dorsey to plead guilty without the benefit of an agreement that, in exchange for a guilty plea, prosecutors would not seek the death penalty; indeed, virtually nothing was done at all by Slusher and McBride to obtain a life sentence for their client. Although they could request funding to hire an investigative team, they declined to hire a dedicated investigator or mitigation specialist, as ABA guidelines recommend in capital cases.

"We know that easy money was top [of] mind for the

lawyers," one *Kansas City Star* editorial suggested, "because one emailed the other and urged him to get on it and request an appointment to the case. Dorsey is 'easy to work with,' he told his friends and 'ready to do what his attorneys advise.' How wonderful of them!"

Megan Crain, a defense attorney later representing Dorsey, said regarding Slusher and McBride's legal representation of their client, "If they had done their basic interviewing of the client and investigation, they would have known that they had a defense, and they would have used that to negotiate either a plea deal with the benefit of a life sentence or they would have gone to trial because they had *a defense*."

A Southern California defense attorney, John Aquilina, recently talked about flat fee representation, "Somebody that's going to put in thousands of hours may generate a dollar an hour. And there's no supervision. There's no restriction. Nobody is telling you you're putting in too many hours or not enough hours." Aquilla added, "It would be a cold day before I take another one." Michael Aed, an attorney in Fresno, California, said that "getting paid on a flat fee would be suicide for my business."

As a result of such exceedingly poor representation and advice by his attorneys, Dorsey pleaded guilty to two counts of first-degree murder. At the plea hearing, Dorsey answered "yes" to the circuit court's question about whether he killed two people and did so after deliberation and knowingly caused their deaths by shooting them. Following the evidentiary hearing, the court held a jury trial for the penalty phase. Dorsey's counsel called nine witnesses, including one expert witness, clinical psychologist Dr. Robert Lee Smith—who completed a psychological summary listing in detail Dorsey's family history, psychiatric history, and substance abuse history. One of Dorsey's family members also testified about his history of mental illness, suicide attempts, and alcohol and drug addictions, all of which was entered into evidence and submitted to the jury.

Dr. Smith first met Dorsey in 2007, during which time they talked about Dorsey's family history but not about the night of the murder. Dr. Smith told Slusher that talking to Dorsey's family might be helpful, but the meeting was never arranged; had the attorney completed work with Dr. Smith, they would have learned that Brian Dorsey had a viable defense to capital first-degree murder, which would have provided a sound basis for seeking an agreement with prosecutors not to pursue the death penalty in exchange for their client's guilty plea. They were unwilling to spend the necessary time to carefully prepare for a guilt or penalty phase trial and, as noted, did not retain a mitigation specialist for assistance in representing Brian Dorsey.

In this case, Slusher and McBride considered the evidence of guilt overwhelming and did not view the facts as favorable to making a diminished capacity argument. They believed that pleading guilty and thereby accepting responsibility was Dorsey's best chance to avoid the death penalty; accordingly, they advised Dorsey to plead guilty.

Slusher testified at a post-conviction evidentiary hearing on 2011, "I think the idea was that we were hoping for some credit acceptance of responsibility... from the jury; they also admitted that they could have asked for money for a fuller and more complete investigation" but said that "dwelling on his [Dorsey's] possible psychosis and other mitigation factors might have undercut their whole strategy: accept blame, express remorse and seek mercy." That strategy, they added at the hearing, was why they encouraged him to plead guilty in the first place. Megan Crane, Co-Director of the MacArthur Justice Center, St. Louis, and an attorney who later represented Dorsey during his appeals process, disagrees completely. "They failed to use a tactic required by ethical standards: demand that prosecutors drop the death penalty in exchange for a guilty plea." Ultimately, the jury must be presented with critical alternative defense strategies.

After pleading guilty, Dr. Smith met with Dorsey again. They discussed the events regarding the night of the murders. Dorsey was diagnosed with a major depressive disorder and recurrent alcohol dependence. Testifying during the penalty phase, Dr. Smith said Dorsey had, for all of his adult life, suffered from an alcohol addiction. Dr Smith said he had also uncovered additional information regarding Dorsey's life. First, Dorsey's mother had a history of depression. Second, some members of his extended family had a history of alcohol abuse. Third, Dorsey's depression predated his drug use.

Dr. Smith added, also during the penalty phase, that Dorsey's depression, by itself, sufficiently diminished his capacity to the extent that he was entirely unable to deliberate properly before killing the Bonnies.

Dr. A.E. Daniel, a forensic psychiatrist, met with Dorsey three times and with his parents for an extensive discussion regarding the night of the murders. Dorsey reported to Dr. Daniel that he remembered being in the bedroom the night of the murders and holding the weapon, but he did not recall the act of shooting the Bonnies.

"Presenting a strong defense during the guilt-innocence phase of the trial," Federal Public Defender Arin Melissa Brenner later wrote, "can also impact the penalty phase by leaving jurors with 'residual doubt' about what happened, if there isn't any concrete proof about what the defendant was thinking about doing at the time of the crime, I have seen that 'residual doubt' can result in life without parole sentences instead of death. Mitigating evidence is critical information, such as evidence of family trauma, addiction, or mental illness, that can reduce a defendant's culpability, a key part of the sentencing phase. Still, it can be introduced during the trial's first phase to give jurors a fuller picture of the events that led to the crime." She added, "Prosecutors portrayed Dorsey as a calculating murderer during the sentencing phase. Slusher and McBride made no effort to counter the government's erroneous assumptions and allegations."

Dorsey, testifying in his defense, said he was sorry for what he had done and also said again he did not remember shooting his cousin, Sarah Bonnie, and her husband, Ben Bonnie because it was during a time when he was high on crack/cocaine and alcohol. He now remembered playing pool and drinking beer with Ben Bonnie and others in Bonnie's garage behind their house in New Bloomfield the night of December 23, 2006; he remembered picking up the shotgun from the garage, carrying and holding the 20-gauge single shot shotgun, but his memory collapsed with no recollection of pulling the trigger or reloading the shotgun or even having sex with Sarah Bonnie, and concluded, "It's been hell for me to know that this has happened and I am responsible for it."

"You are kind of getting the jury ready to hear about what went wrong here," Arin Melissa Brenner explained to *HuffPost*. "Yes, maybe they are guilty, but you are framing how the jury should receive all the information they are about to get overloaded with—and that's especially true for experts. Introducing a lot of brain science to jurors helps pave the way for the guilt phase; it is readily more understandable in the penalty phase."

On April 28, 2008, the jury found seven aggravating factors and returned a verdict recommending that Brian Dorsey be sentenced to death for the two murders. Concerning the murder of Benjamin Bonnie, the jury found three aggravating circumstances:

1. That the murder of Benjamin Bonnie was committed while the defendant was engaged in the commission of another unlawful homicide of Sarah Bonnie.
2. That the defendant murdered Benjamin Bonnie for the defendant to receive money or any other thing of monetary value from Benjamin Bonnie.
3. That the murder of Benjamin Bonnie involved depravity of mind and, as a result thereof, the murder was outrageously vile, horrible, and inhuman.

Concerning the murder of Sarah Bonnie, the jury found four aggravating circumstances:

1. That the murder of Sarah Bonnie was committed while the defendant was engaged in the commission of another unlawful homicide of Benjamin Bonnie.
2. That the defendant murdered Sarah Bonnie to receive money or any other thing of monetary value.
3. That the murder of Sarah Bonnie involved depravity of mind, and as a result thereof, the murder was outrageously and wantonly vile, horrible, and inhuman.
4. That the murder of Sarah Bonnie was committed while the defendant was in the perpetration of rape.

According to the court, the evidence supported each of the aggravating factors found by the jury. There was no dispute that Brian Dorsey killed each victim while engaging in the homicide of the other. There was also strong evidence that Dorsey killed Sarah and Ben Bonnie for pecuniary/money gain; after killing Sarah and Ben, Dorsey took many of their belongings in a hopeless attempt to pay his drug debts. There was some evidence supporting a finding that Dorsey also committed rape.

The Circuit Court of Boone County sentenced Dorsey accordingly. During cross-examination, Dorsey had said he did not care if the jury recommended the death penalty or life in prison without the possibility of parole.

When contacted by *CNN*, Christopher Slusher declined to comment, and the other attorney, Scott McBride, did not immediately respond. However, in a previous appeal, both lawyers testified that the flat fee did not affect their decisions in the case, and both knew they could have requested more money if they needed it. Nevertheless, his more recent lawyers made discoveries about Dorsey's past that his original flat fee lawyers might have brought to the jury had they sought money for investigators, which almost certainly would have resulted in a more comprehensive and more effective representation for their client, Brian Dorsey.

"At the time, none of us on the Court knew how compromised and ineffective his trial lawyers were," Former Chief Justice of the Missouri Supreme Court Michael A. Wolff said.

Megan Crane said, "To prove first-degree murder, prosecutors must prove murders were carried out with deliberation, meaning there was 'cool reflection for any length of time no matter how brief,' according to state statute. But Dorsey was 'neurologically incapable of deliberation because of the psychosis.'"

"Death sentence[s] imposed under these conditions often says more about the external funding limitations placed on counsel and less about the nature of the crime or the culpability of the defendant," said Emily Olson-Gault, director of the American Bar Association's Death Penalty Representation Project.

On July 16, 2010, the Supreme Court of Missouri affirmed the trial court's death penalty sentence for Brian Dorsey.

Kent Denzel of the Missouri Public Defender's Office in Columbia appeared before the Supreme Court on December 4, 2013, arguing for a stay of execution for death row inmate Brian Dorsey. He questioned whether or not Sarah Bonnie was raped before her death. In a brief with the Court, Denzel also questioned the effectiveness of Dorsey's flat fee attorneys, who did not thoroughly investigate Dorsey's mental health or history of substance abuse. However, the Court then reaffirmed the Circuit Court's decision.

It was December 13, 2023, when the Supreme Court issued a warrant for the execution of Brian Dorsey and ordered Dorsey's previously imposed death penalty to be carried out on April 9, 2024. Subsequently, Dorsey filed three separate petitions for a writ of habeas corpus claiming: (1) he was innocent of the first-degree murder offenses he pleaded guilty to committing because he was incapable of deliberation at the time of the offenses due to his drug-induced psychosis; (2) he was denied effective trial counsel due to a flat fee arrangement that created a conflict of interest; and (3) his execution would violate the Eighth Amendment because he belongs to a unique class of persons to whom the penological goals are no longer met.

The Court denied all three petitions and said Dorsey does not deny that he committed the murders and has not established that he is innocent of first-degree murder. The Court previously denied Dorsey's claim of ineffective counsel, stating it lacked merit, and Dorsey was procedurally barred from raising this claim again in his writ petition.

Finally, the Court said Dorsey's Eighth Amendment claim was without merit and, ultimately, a plea for clemency was beyond the Court's review and authority. Dorsey's offenses—two counts of first-degree murder—were not disproportionate to capital punishment. Additionally, the Court said, Dorsey did not possess a characteristic *at the time of the offense* that made the death penalty a disproportionately harsh punishment. The jury had found seven aggravating factors warranting the imposition of the death penalty for a writ of habeas corpus.

Megan G. Crane filed, on December 29, 2023, an 80-page writ of habeas petition that said, "Dorsey was experiencing drug psychosis the night of the crime and thus incapable of deliberation—the requisite for capital murder. Instead, he should have been charged with second-degree murder, making him ineligible for the death penalty." His defense attorneys pressured him to plead guilty in exchange for nothing. Slusher and McBride could have also requested additional funding to staff their team. Still, they declined to hire a dedicated investigator or mitigation specialist as ABA guidelines recommend in capital cases. Ultimately, this meant the jury was never presented with an alternative—much less the truth—that Brian Dorsey was experiencing drug psychosis and was, therefore, not guilty of first-degree murder.

Incredibly, his flat-fee attorneys did not ask their client for details about the night of the crime. The flat-fee payment plan for defense disincentivized the work needed in capital casework, and the petition contends that is why his attorneys had him plead guilty without a guarantee of a life sentence; that the flat-fee attorneys did not adequately investigate the alternative of pleading second-degree murder, which would almost certainly have resulted in a life sentence without parole; and discussed his deep shame and remorse have shaped him and the way he lives daily with deep regret. The petition also notes, "Many people are forever grieving the loss of Sarah and Ben Bonnie. We recognize that no words or efforts can make this tragedy less painful; were Dorsey's sentence to be commuted, he would like to continue his work in prison as a barber, [and that] his Sunday phone calls and his conversations with family making life meaningful enough to make life worth living."

On March 24, 2024, the final decision was made. The Supreme Court of Missouri again affirmed the sentence of Brian Joseph Dorsey as death—with the execution date of April 9, 2024, using a lethal injection of pentobarbital at the Eastern Reception and Corrections Center's execution chamber.

On April 1, 2024, Brian Dorsey's attorneys filed a petition for writ of certiorari with the United States Supreme Court, asking the court to determine whether the flat fee paid to the appointed public defenders created an actual conflict of interest that violated his Sixth Amendment right to effective counsel. The petition was denied.

QUOTE FROM JUSTICE MICHAEL A. WOLFF

"At the time none of us on the Court were aware of
how compromised and ineffective his trial lawyers
were."

**Michael W. Wolff
Former Chief Justice, Supreme Court of Missouri**

POTOSI CORRECTIONAL CENTER

"I don't know if I have even seen a record as good as his!"

Troy Steele, former Potosi Prison Warden

"If Brian Dorsey has not been rehabilitated, then the word ceases to have any meaning."

Potosi prison correctional staff

"When you are with Brian, you know he has changed."

Potosi prison correctional staff

FOLLOWING BOONE COUNTY CIRCUIT COURT'S sentencing trial in July 2010, Dorsey was given two death sentences. He was then transferred to Potosi Correctional Center in Mineral Point, Missouri, a town in Washington

County with a population outside the prison of 351. The Potosi center houses about 800 death row, maximum-security, high-risk inmates. In this facility, prisoners under the death sentence are allowed to integrate with other prisoners. Within the prison, death row inmates are referred to as capital punishment inmates with access to the law library, meals with other inmates, and courtyard privileges, once each day for exercise. These inmates, such as Brian Dorsey, may have exceptional custody levels, minimum custody, medium custody, close custody, and administrative segregation.

After a year, Dorsey was moved to the honor dorm section of the prison, which is a special housing area for inmates who continually demonstrated good conduct and no behavior problems. The dorm is designed to reward positive behavior and encourage a more rehabilitative environment. Inmates in the honor dorm typically have access to better living conditions and more privileges compared to the Potosi prison general population—in some situations, this approach has provided some lower recidivism rates. However, despite this special assignment, Dorsey was nevertheless a part of the everyday prison population.

Dorsey lived in Potosi for 17 years with a spotless disciplinary record. He worked as a barber for the wardens, corrections staff, and chaplains for 11 years, where he was entrusted with equipment that could be used to harm prison staff. The prison staff clearly trusted him in that they put themselves in a position of vulnerability when sitting in the barber chair. He saw his work as a barber as an opportunity to give back, create positivity, and perhaps provide a light in someone's day. He was also allowed to play baseball with other prisoners, demonstrating the level of staff trust he was given since he was permitted to use a baseball bat close to prison staff members.

In an interview with *The Marshall Project*, Megan Crane, Dorsey's attorney, said, "Her client wants to find a way to make people's lives better to atone for what he had done."

BRIAN DORSEY'S FAMILY: THE DEATH SENTENCE

"We are living in the middle of an eye-for-an-eye country, but I wish people would understand it's not that black and white."

Jenni Gerhauser

"I believe in the death penalty, and I think he deserves it!"

Jacob Bonnie
Ben Bonnie's father

"IT IS A UNIQUE, INCREDIBLY TRAGIC EXPERIENCE because you are on both sides of the story," Dorsey's life-time close friend, Jenni Gerhauser, who is also related to one of the victims, Sarah Bonnie, said. "There is nothing positive about this awful, regrettable situation; there simply is not. They are planning to execute Brian, and, in my opinion, that is cruel and unusual punishment."

Growing up, Jennie Gerhauser and Brian Dorsey were

always close. They were born about three weeks apart; they spent holidays, birthdays, and most summers together. Many family members, including some related to Sarah Bonnie, have supported the ongoing clemency petitions submitted to the courts in a concerted effort not to execute Brian. Most of the family knew that Brian struggled throughout his life with extremely severe depression beginning at an early age.

Backed by her three cousins, Gail Thompson said her family does not need to experience more death. She said, "Brian Dorsey would never have committed the crime if he was in his right mind; our love for him does not so blind us that we don't understand that he was convicted of a terrible crime against someone we loved just as much as we have loved Brian." She added, "But we are not capable of rewriting history and convincing ourselves that Brian still isn't the same loving, compassionate, helpful person he always was."

"He was completely out of control, obviously not in this right mind. When he committed the murders." Dorsey's cousin Jenni added, "When you were with Brian, you are better, you feel protected, you feel loved; to have him taken away like this would be very hard." Another family member said, "Brian was convicted of a terrible crime; we have never denied that, but Brian is not the worst of the worst. A single terrible night would not justify killing him." Jenni added, "We live in the middle of an eye-for-an-eye country, but I wish people would understand, it's simply not that black and white." In defending Brian, she acknowledged, "I've lost half of my family."

Others in the family had strong feelings in the other direction. Some hoped the governor would allow the execution to proceed. "After years of grief and suffering, there may be some light at the end of the tunnel," one Bonnie family member said before the final Supreme Court decision. "Dorsey will now get some of the justice Sarah and Ben Bonnie deserve; his crime left their daughter, Jade Bonnie, without parents."

As the years continued after that fateful night in late December 2006, the remaining family members did what they could to keep memories of Ben and Sarah alive for Jade, sometimes taking her to the cemetery to release great numbers of multi-colored balloons into the sky in her parents' memory.

One family member wrote, "We think of the things Jade has missed [experiencing with] her parents. There would be the first day of school, then school parties, first dates, simply finding herself at the great age of sixteen, maybe a first boyfriend, and then her high school graduation, perhaps college, and also life beyond that to maybe marriage and children of her own without two of their grandparents."

Another family member said, "All of this was taken from her by a family member who said he loved and cared for her. Jacob Bonnie was thirty when his younger brother, Ben Bonnie, was murdered. Ben Bonnie was his best friend, to me somebody like that does not deserve to wake up... I believe in the death penalty, and I think he deserves it. The things I heard from the detectives and stuff weren't very pleasant. To stab someone in the back who brought you in to help you out... the betrayal. That betrayal I'll never forgive." He added, "It was mostly hard on my parents to have a child die before you do. It is just out of sequence. For every holiday, we have two empty chairs."

Jacob Bonnie reflected for a moment when talking with a reporter and said, my "two sons would have loved their Uncle Ben Bonnie, definitely a family man who spent time with his family and on camping trips and motorcycle rides. The punishment will fit the crime in this case, and it's nice to see the ball finally start to roll on the execution; for a while, you almost wonder if they forgot."

Despite the abject horror of the murders, Brian Dorsey, on death row and in prison, has been able to remain in contact with some family members by letters and telephone, but not in person.

"Except for his parents, who have now died," Megan Crane reported, "Brian Dorsey does not allow family members to visit him. By not seeing family members, he hopes, in some way, to minimize the harm his own death could cause." She added, "He thinks he has caused them enough harm and wants to create some distance between them."

THE EFFORT TO SAVE THE LIFE OF BRIAN DORSEY

"From my perspective, after decades in prison, I do not hesitate to say that Brian Dorsey would be a pointless cruelty; he deserves Governor Parson's mercy."

Timothy Lancaster.
Potosi Correctional Center

"Contact Parson and tell him to stay Dorsey's execution, citing Catholic teaching on the inadmissibility of the death penalty!"

Catholic Bishops of Missouri

"Governor Parson has chosen to ignore the wealth of information before him, showing him that Brian Dorsey is uniquely deserving of mercy."

Megan Crane
MacArthur Justice Center, St. Louis

ON DECEMBER 13, 2023, THE DAY AFTER REVEREND Matt Friedrich of Kirkwood, Missouri, decided to serve as Brian Dorsey's spiritual advisor in prison, the day after the Supreme Court of Missouri handed down the decision that Brian Dorsey would be executed on April 9, 2024, Reverend Friedrich remembers that "everything became a lot more urgent."

Friedrich and Dorsey formed a close bond, and Friedrich was incredulous when he learned that Dorsey, who had spent over 17 years in prison under a death sentence, would ultimately be executed.

"The execution process itself is grotesque," Friedrich said. "To be able to be with someone, that is what we do, you think about life's trajectory, and, you know, imagining at that time you had no idea where life would go, it's a strange thing, it feels like the world would stop if we were going to do these things [executions]..."

The case drew national attention when hundreds voiced their opinions and requested Governor Parson grant amnesty to a completely rehabilitated prisoner facing execution, and allow him to serve out his life in prison.

Five jurors from the court's criminal sentencing phase said Dorsey should be granted amnesty. A former Chief Justice of the Missouri Supreme Court, and Republican State Representatives Tony Lovasco of O'Fallon, Jeff Coleman of Grain Valley, and Adam Schwadron of St. Charles, said, "Dorsey is uniquely qualified for our mercy and should not be executed."

"He has spent every day of the last 18 years trying to make up for the single act of violence," attorney Kirk Henderson said. "Executing Brian Dorsey is a pointless cruelty, an exercise of the State's power that serves no legitimate penological process... the penological goal of rehabilitation has been satisfied, and an execution does not meet the constitutionally required goals of retribution and deterrence."

In a letter to the governor, former Chief Justice of the Missouri Supreme Court Michael A. Wolff added that a Dorsey execution would represent "a rare failing of the legal system itself" and "will dishonor our system of capital punishment."

Congresswoman Cori Bush asked Governor Parson to stop the scheduled execution of convicted killer Brian Dorsey. She said, "Experts concluded that Dorsey was in a drug-induced psychosis at the time of the murders."

The Missouri Department of Corrections staff members understand "that they could be jeopardizing their career by supporting clemency, yet scores have done just that," one source said.

Among those asking Missouri's governor to spare the life of Brian Dorsey were several Catholic bishops, law professors, hundreds of police and prison officers, and members from many national mental health organizations. One wrote, "By the grace of God, I hope you will find your way to give him a life sentence instead of death."

The support for Dorsey's compassion extended far beyond corrections officials. Hundreds joined an extraordinarily massive chorus involving hundreds of voices, urging Governor Parson to stop the scheduled execution of convicted killer Brian Dorsey, emphasizing that experts concluded he was in a drug-induced psychosis at the time of the murders.

One hundred fifty former and current Missouri

Department of Corrections employees signed a letter to the governor requesting that he commute Dorsey's sentence to life in prison without parole. They wrote, "We are part of the law enforcement community who believe in law and order. We believe in the use of capital punishment. But we agree that the death penalty is not the appropriate punishment for Brian Dorsey, who had stayed out of trouble, has never gotten himself into any situations, and has been respectful of us and his fellow inmates."

One prison staff member wrote, "If Brian Dorsey has not been rehabilitated, then the word ceases to have any meaning at all." Another wrote, "The Brian Dorsey I have known for years could not hurt anyone; he does not deserve to be executed." Another staff member wrote, "It is my impression that he has spent his time since [his imprisonment] trying to do his best by being a role model to other inmates and providing a valuable lesson to staff."

Other prison staff letters shared:

"Over my time at DOC, I have met many inmates, but I have never written a letter like this. I do not take writing a letter like this lightly. When you spend time around Brian, you know he has changed; we trusted him with scissors to cut our hair, which says a lot about Brian. I am a person who respects law and order. I do not take this letter lightly. The Brian I have known for years could not hurt anyone. The Brian I know does not deserve to be executed."

"Not only has law and order been my life's work... I believe in capital punishment... but the death penalty is not the appropriate punishment for Brian Dorsey—a role model for other prisoners. I watched Mr. Dorsey during his court hearings and observed him struggle with the pain he has caused his parents and his family. If you ask me, if it were not for drugs, this would never have happened."

"I have encountered some prison inmates who are not rehabilitated and others who are. Brian Dorsey fits the description of the latter category. I know that he is very sorry for his crime. Brian demonstrates a spirit of remorse and regret. Brian's remorse is genuine and always present. Brian does a good job and is an asset to the prison and the state of his employment as the prison barber. I believe that Brian must have been very high on drugs and out of his right mind to have committed murders or even to have caused harm to another person."

"I believe in our correctional system, and I believe in capital punishment, but I do not believe that Mr. Dorsey should be executed. He has accepted what he did and taken accountability for his crime. I think he has spent his time trying his best by being a role model to other inmates and providing valuable service to the staff. He is an example of what we want inmates to be."

"I have learned that Brian is different in a couple of ways. The first thing that stands out is that in all the years we have been here (at Potosi Correctional Center), Brian has never caused a problem, and Brian has never been written up. Not even once. Aside from staying out of trouble, I cannot think of another inmate with that record. He is always respectful. He is always kind. People who no longer work here at Potosi Correctional Center will return to get a haircut from Brian. I believe actions have consequences. I believe that Brian deserves to spend the rest of his life in prison for what he did. However, I do not want to see him executed; he is very sorry for and remorseful about his crime."

Others also wrote in support of Brian Dorsey:

In a review of Dorsey's prison record, Troy Steel, former Potosi warden, wrote that "Dorsey was a model inmate housed in the honor dorm." Steel added, "I don't know if I have ever seen a record as good as his; that is extraordinary, especially in a prison environment where people are sometimes problematic or have to defend themselves. I have no reason to believe that should his sentence be commuted, his behavior would... change in any way." During 17 years of facing capital punishment, Steel wrote, Dorsey never had "a single infraction, a rare feat in a place where guards can issue an infraction for something as minor as the tone of voice of a prisoner or the number of pieces of paper in a cell." In an interview with the *Kansas City Star,* Steel said, "He is in one of the most trusted places in the institution, being the staff barber."

"The very concept of corrections," David Lancaster, a Missouri attorney and former corrections officer, wrote, "implies that we want incarcerated people to change their ways. Executing Brian Dorsey would dishonor his hard work to fulfill that objective. At the same time, taking Dorsey's life would be especially traumatic to former and current Potosi staff members; executing Brian will do nothing to promote public safety." Another wrote, "I spent 27 years as a correctional officer and investigator in the Missouri Department of Corrections, including many years at Potosi Correctional Center. I consider myself to be a law-and-order conservative, and I support the death penalty. But I, along with more than 70 current and former Missouri correctional officers, cannot support the execution of Brian Dorsey." David Lancaster added, "I saw Dorsey's hardworking humility personally up close—not just because he was housed in the honor dorm at Potosi, but because he has served as the prison barber for over a decade. This position, in which he cuts the hair and trims the beards of prison staff—even Wardens Troy Steele and Don Roper— reflects the trust and respect entrusted to him. Many of us wouldn't let anyone else do the job once he started cutting our hair. Mr. Dorsey is an excellent barber and a kind and respectful man."

Prison official Warden Steel shared that, with an inmate as popular and respected as Dorsey was, his execution could very well traumatize a number of prison staff members. Letters from prison staff members to the governor show that "his execution would be at odds with one's moral convictions." In a prison system faced with high turnover, "this type of trauma will almost certainly lead some prison staff members to leave this type of work altogether." The significant impact on Potosi staff members can, in some situations, lead even to PTSD or other psychiatric difficulties, including symptoms of acute stress disorder. Concerning executions, the risk of enduring harmful consequences expands to include those in prison death roles who have had prolonged contact with the inmate to be executed. In short, "executing Brian Dorsey would emotionally harm the Potosi staff and also could lead to the prison being less safe for both the prison staff and the incarcerated there." This is "especially relevant to Brian Dorsey's situation given the widespread positive reaction to him among prison employees and fellow inmates."

The emotional impact of the death penalty generally reaches far beyond those in the official capacity who carry out or witness the executions and includes other personnel —this trauma is part of every execution. Missouri Department of Corrections officials already knew that the execution of Brian Dorsey would be incredibly traumatic to prison staff. When they couldn't stop the execution, correction officials at least changed the execution site from the Potosi Correctional Center to the Eastern Reception, Diagnostic and Correctional Center in Bonne Terre, Missouri.

The advocacy of so many corrections officials on behalf of Mr. Dorsey "is really remarkable," said Robin M. Maher, director of the Death Penalty Information Center. "I have never seen any other case with this kind of support from current and former corrections staff. This is unprecedented because (the officers) also are putting themselves on the line by signing these letters. This is truly extraordinary, and it goes to the character of Mr. Dorsey... they truly believe that Brian Dorsey deserves clemency and that he is someone who should not be facing execution,"

Michele Smith, Co-Director of the Missourians to Abolish the Death Penalty said, "The flood of support for Dorsey's clemency is very significant." This group circulated a petition for clemency that argued that killing Dorsey "does nothing to promote public safety and only serves to create further harm."

Timothy Lancaster, a former officer at the prison where Dorsey was held, said, "From my perspective, after decades in corrections, I do not hesitate to say that executing Brian Dorsey would be a pointless cruelty. He is a good man who deserves Governor Parson's mercy. If granted pardon, I am confident that he will spend the rest of his life continuing to follow the path of transformation he has pursued faithfully for the past 17 years."

DEATH OF THE PERFECT PRISONER

"He is struggling with as much shame
and remorse as the likelihood that he is going to die in a
few days."

Megan Crane
Co-Director of the MacArthur Justice Center, St. Louis

"I am totally, overwhelmingly sorry!"

Brian Dorsey

"There are rare cases where those of us who sit in judg-
ment of a man convicted of capital murder got it wrong.
The decision affirming Brian Dorsey's death sentence is
just such a case."

Michael W. Wolff

Former Chief Justice, Supreme Court of Missouri

JONATHON SHIFLET, GOVERNOR MIKE L. PARSON'S office spokesman, said on Wednesday, April 7, 2024, that the governor and his legal team were reviewing the Dorsey file. Parson had served as Missouri governor since 2018. In this position, he had the authority to grant reprieves, computations, and pardons; he had never commuted a death penalty case—12 prisoners had died by lethal injection since 2018. The Missouri Probation and Parole Board issued non-binding, non-public recommendations to Parson, who decided after each case has been fully adjudicated. Parson denied Dorsey's separate plea for clemency.

Missouri executes more prisoners than nearly all other U.S. states, with 91 persons executed since 1976, the only exceptions are Texas, Oklahoma, Virginia, and Florida.

Missouri Attorney General Andrew Bailey, who advocated the death penalty for Dorsey, said the Missouri Supreme Court had reviewed Dorsey's convictions and sentences. The United States District Court for the Western District of Missouri, the United States Court of Appeals for the Eighth Circuit, and the United States Supreme Court had also reviewed those convictions and sentences. According to the Death Penalty Information Organization, Dorsey would be the 13th inmate put to death under Parson and the 101st inmate to die since Missouri reinstated the death penalty in a 1989 clemency application. This was Bailey's first death penalty case.

In a motion filed on April 8, a group of attorneys, working pro bono, argued that the head of the Missouri Department of Corrections, Trevor Foley, should not be allowed to oversee Dorsey's execution. Parson had appointed Foley on November 30, 2023, a man with experience working as a budget analyst for the state. Dorsey's attorneys argued that Foley had no experience in his current position since it requires overseeing the selection of the confidential execution team and the implementation of the lethal injection protocol, with the attendant possibility of "a substantial risk of serious, tortured and psychological pain."

According to state law, "The director shall have the education, training, and experience in correctional management." The director also oversees the selection of the confidential execution team and the implementation of the precise lethal injection protocol. In their clemency petition, Despite this petition, Foley remained in office.

Dorsey's legal team also argued again that "Dorsey was in a state of drug psychosis the night of the double murder and was incapable of deliberation—years of substance abuse aimed at self-medicating chronic depression— making him ineligible for a first-degree murder charge."

Prior to this, the Supreme Court of Missouri denied Dorsey's last appeal on Wednesday, April 3, six days before his scheduled execution. Also on April 3, Dorsey was transferred to the Eastern Reception, Diagnostic and Correctional Center in Bonne Terre, Missouri, south of St Louis. This center, with a prison population of 2,500, is administered by the Missouri Department of Corrections and serves as the execution point for male offenders in eastern Missouri. It contains Missouri's lethal execution chamber. Severe staffing shortages at that facility have resulted in inmates being held on extended and frequent lockdowns, unable to leave their cells even for medical appointments.

Dorsey was placed in solitary confinement for the next six days in a small, sparingly furnished, windowless cell awaiting execution; he was facing the state-specified lethal injection protocol—with, his attorneys argued, "possibility of a substantial risk of serious, tortured and psychological pain."

In a separate filing with the U.S. District Court of Eastern Missouri, Federal Public Defender Arin Melissa Brenner argued that the injection process would cause Dorsey to be in "significant pain and anguish," and render him "unable to concentrate on seeking repentance, a violation of his religious beliefs and First Amendment rights." In other words, his freedom of religion would be abridged, including the administration of the last rites. Brenner continued, "There is simply no justification for some of [the lethal injection] actions, which cause excruciating pain, including just moments before all people must engage in the most important spiritual and religious practices of their lives—preparing souls for the afterlife." The Missouri Attorney General's office did not respond.

Brenner asked that "Dorsey be given drugs to ease the process of death from a phenobarbital injection, which has been shown to cause instant filling of the lungs," possibly fentanyl, morphine, or a general anesthetic. The motion also asked for a temporary restraining order and preliminary injunction requesting that the court put a hold on Dorsey's execution while considering these arguments. Finally, she argued that the state's protocols violate the protection against cruel and unusual punishment. The protocol offers no guidance on how far the execution team can go to find a suitable vein, leaving open the possibility of an invasive cut-down procedure, involving an incision and forceps to pull away tissue from an interior vein to access it. Her petition continued, stating that "Dorsey had a higher-than-normal risk of needing a cutdown because he was obese." Also, Dorsey's veins might be compromised because he had diabetes and was a former IV drug user.

Missouri's execution protocol allows for "surgery without anesthesia." The state's official instructions provide that "medical personnel shall determine the most appropriate intravenous (IV) line locations. A primary IV line and a secondary IV shall be inserted unless the prisoner's physical condition makes inserting more than one IV unduly difficult. Medical personnel may insert the primary IV line as a peripheral or central venous line, provided they have appropriate training, education, and experience." Missouri's complete execution process is largely secret, and it is difficult to tell if and how often cutdown procedures are necessary. If the typical protocol process of finding a suitable vein to inject the lethal drug did not work correctly, at that point, attorneys for Dorsey said they would begin an appeal aimed at saving his life.

"Medication would be inadequate, and if the process is necessary, Dorsey should be given a local anesthetic," Megan Crane said, "it is excruciating. Even if given oral pain relief or opioids, that will not relieve the pain."

A spokesperson for Attorney General Andrew Bailey did not comment but referred to the state's response to the appeal: "Cut-down procedures are rarely used under Missouri's execution protocol. And if a cut-down procedure was necessary, medical personnel could access pain-relieving medications."

It was early afternoon on Tuesday, April 9, 2024, when

the U.S. Supreme Court finally rejected Dorsey's final appeals, with no dissents recorded. His final meal was served at 11:00 a.m. His menu included two bacon double cheeseburgers, two chicken strips, two large orders of fries, and a pizza topped with sausage, pepperoni, onion, mushrooms, and extra cheese.

The U.S. Supreme Court, within the last few years, ruled that spiritual advisors could pray and touch prisoners during their last moments during the execution process. Following his last meal, he met with Reverend Friedrich for about an hour, during which they laughed and cried, told stories, talked about family and memories, and spoke at some length about what would happen after Brian Dorsey's death—Dorsey was uncertain about the unknown terrain after death and what all of it might mean after nearly a generation in prison, Dorsey had often thought about how the Bible was created and what it really meant to have a relationship with God.

"I think," in general, Reverend Friedrich said, "the way the church manifests itself is not always looking for people who do not fit in, and I think Brian felt that way."

As far as Brian Dorsey's last days, Megan Crane said, "As the execution has drawn closer, Mr. Dorsey has tried to manage his expectations from the courts or the governor. He has taken full responsibility since day one, and the horror that he could have done this is still his focus in this final week; he is struggling with as much shame and remorse as the likelihood that he is going to die in a few days."

Dorsey himself, in a final written statement, again expressed remorse and sorrow for the killings: "To all my family and loved ones I share with Sarah and to all the surviving loved ones of Ben, I am totally, overwhelmingly sorry. Words cannot judge the weight of my guilt and shame... to my family and friends who tried to prevent this, I am grateful to you, I love you... I carry no ill will or anger, only acceptance and understanding."

THE EXECUTION

Missouri's Execution Chamber includes three rooms.

Execution Room: This is where the inmate is strapped to a gurney. This room has the medical equipment necessary for the complete execution procedure.

Observation Room: Adjacent to the execution room, curtains in this room remain closed during the execution process.

Control Room: The room for the execution teams and the equipment to administer lethal injections.

Missouri's lethal injection process follows a series of regulated steps to ensure that the execution process is carried out according to law and procedure:

Preparation: Dorsey was moved to a holding cell next to the execution chamber. He was strip-searched, then secured with upper and lower restraints to the execution table and moved into the execution chamber. Leads from an electrograph were attached to his chest. He was observed from a separate room as well as with the help of a high-resolution camera and microphone.

Next, following procedure, execution team members located two veins and carefully placed two catheters and a backup into his body. The catheters were connected to the observation room and put into a medication delivery unit called a manifold.

Chemical Preparation:

Medical personnel prepared the chemicals:

Syringes 1 & 2: (5) grams of phenobarbital

Syringe 3: (30 cc) of saline solution

Syringes 4 & 5: additional grams of phenobarbital

Syringe 6: (30 cc) of saline solution

Drug Administration: The lethal injection follows a three-drug protocol:

A sedative to render the inmate unconscious.

A paralytic agent to stop all muscle movement.

Potassium Chloride to stop all heart activity.

Witnesses: By the time the witnesses arrived, Dorsey was already strapped to the gurney, and the IV line had already been set, generally known as the most challenging part of the execution process.

A state-approved group of witnesses, including media and legal officials and family members of the victims and the inmate, entered the execution viewing area at the Eastern Reception, Diagnostic and Correctional Center. Before the next steps in the process began, Dorsey saw the witnesses and slightly smiled when he saw his legal team wearing matching maroon T-shirts emblazoned with a white heart.

Reporter Moore added that Reverend Friedrich was not allowed in the execution chamber until the preparation was complete. "The thing I told him," Friedrich said, by then allowed in the execution chamber close enough to Brian to touch his shoulder, "over and over again as he was dying is that 'love you, Brian, and God loves you,' and hopefully that is the last thing he heard."

A few minutes after the phenobarbital was injected, Dorsey took a few deep breaths, then several shallow, quick breaths. At one point, he raised his head from the pillow and blinked hard before all movement stopped. Death occurred at 6:11 p.m. after a single dose injection. The viewing area curtains remained closed while staff members checked Dorsey's vital signs. Missouri protocol calls for medical personnel on the execution team to check whether a prisoner is dead after a sufficient amount of time—generally about five minutes. They reopened the observation area curtains, and a white sheet was placed over him up to his face.

Karen Pojman, Communications Director for the Missouri Department of Corrections, said no cutdown procedure was necessary for Brian Dorsey. "It went smoothly with no problems."

Concerning the actual execution process, Bob Priddy, former News Director for the statewide radio network Missouri Net, had witnessed 22 executions, including two phenobarbital-only executions, exactly like Brian Dorsey's (but did not attend Dorsey's), and said, "I have never seen any discomfort. Usually, a news media witness will get a call from the attorney general's office, probably a day or so after an execution, asking if we had seen any signs of panic, pain, or struggles or anything like that, and the answer he always gives—no, the prisoner just went to sleep. There is seldom anything to talk about an execution except to say the inmate was executed, might have gasped a few times, then was silent and pronounced dead in a few minutes. There is nothing especially dramatic about it; it is very clinical. The entire process must be completed entirely free of cruel and unusual punishment as the Constitution requires."

In June 2024, two months after the Dorsey execution, Reverend Jeff Hood, known as a death row minister, who had witnessed six executions in other venues, noticed the Missouri execution chamber and the window of the Missouri death chamber were one-way, meaning witnesses could see the inmate, but the inmate cannot see who is watching them. Reverend Hood said, It's like a house of horrors: very bizarre. "Witnessing executions," he said, "makes him feel like a murderer. I'm called to be there for my guy. I'm called to pray and read scripture. For all my good intentions, I ultimately do nothing to stop it... I sit there and watch someone I love be murdered. In my inaction, I join the team of murderers; being part of the entire process is moral torture."

Pronouncement of Death: After death is confirmed, the body is then prepared for release to the family or for burial. The process is designed to be as humane and efficient as possible, though it remains a deeply controversial and emotionally charged practice.

The governor's office released a statement: "The pain Dorsey brought to others can never be rectified, but carrying out Dorsey's sentence according to law and the Court's order will deliver justice and provide closure."

Co-Director of Missourians for Abolishing the Death Penalty, Elyse Max, said, "Many people are against abolishing the death penalty because they're concerned about victims and [those] who are impacted by first-degree murder. What we saw today with the Dorsey family is that it just keeps the trauma on families for decades after a crime happens."

Postscript: Some officials refer to the peace of mind that executions give to the families of homicide victims. Indeed, some gain some sense of closure and justice; many do not. Inevitably, as time passes, there is a profound sense of loss suffered by the loved ones of death row inmates who didn't want to see their friend or family member die, no matter how horrendous their actions.

For whatever reasons known only to him, Governor Parson decided to ignored hundreds of requests for mercy, disregarded an extraordinarily flawless prison record, and overlooked completely obvious rehabilitation. All things considered, Brian Dorsey's execution has the appearance of a homicide.

BIBLIOGRAPHY

MEDIA/REPORTERS

Andone, Dakin, "Advocates for Missouri death row inmate Brian Dorsey plead for clemency with days to go before his execution" April 7, 2024.

Andone, Dakin, "Missouri executes Brian Dorsey for 2006 double murder after mercy bid backed by 72 correctional officers," CNN Apr. 10, 2024

Bailey, Andrew, Missouri Attorney General

Brash, Ben, "Missouri executes Brian Dorsey despite pleas from 70 prison guards." The Washington Post, April 9, 2024.

Brenner, Arin Melissa, Brian Dorsey Vandergriff Civil Case No 15-08000 (Western District of Missouri).

Burdziak, Alan. "Attorney for death row inmate focuses on DNA evidence," Columbia Daily Tribune. December 5, 2013.

Coen, Susie. "Why 60 prison guards don't want a double murderer to be executed," The Telegraph, January 25, 2004.

"Cori Bush asking to stop the execution of Brian Dorsey," KTVI St Louis

DeFede, Jim, "Cori Bush asking to stop execution of Brian Dorsey," CBS NEWS MIAMI April 4, 2024.

Gomez, Julia. "Model inmate: Missouri correction officer seeks death penalty reprieve for Brian Dorsey," USA Today, January 2024.

"He Faces Execution. His Lawyers May Have Earned Less Than $4 per hour." The Marshal Project, April 3, 2024

Henneberger, Melinda, "Don't execute Brian Dorsey. His flat-fee lawyers had all the wrong incentives—opinion," Kansas City Star, April 4, 2024.

Hickey, Christoper, & Dakin, Andone & Will Mullery, "What happens during a typical three-drug lethal injection." CNN, November 28, 2023.

Lancaster, Timothy, "We correction officers know Brian Dorsey has changed. Gov. Parson doesn't execute him. Opinion," Kansas City Star, April 1, 2024

Matthew Sanders," Man scheduled to die for killing cousins in Callaway

County seeks to halt execution," ABC 17, Fox 22 KQFX, February 13, 2024

Maylee, Chief Deputy Darryl, Crime Scene Report, Dec 23, 2006

Meyer, Joe, "Killer doesn't recall shootings," Columbia Daily Tribune, August 28, 2008.

Meyers, Amanda Lee & James Powell, "Comforting the condemned: Inside the execution chamber with reverend focused on humanity," USA Today June 16, 2024

"Missouri governor denies clemency for a man scheduled for execution on Tuesday," U.S. News, December 12, 2024

"Missouri Governor Denies Clemency to Death Row Inmate Despite Catholic Protests," National Catholic Reporter, November 23, 2024

"Missouri's First Execution of 2024 Scheduled for Man Whose Trial Lawyers Had Conflicts of Interest and Who Has Unprecedented Support of Clemency." Death Penalty Information Center, September 25, 2024

Moore, Katie, "Attorney say Missouri correction director unqualified to oversee execution next month," Kansas City Star, Mar.30, 2006.

Moore, Katie, "In a rare move, 60 Missouri prison staffers advocate for commuting man's death sentence," Kansas City Star, Jan. 22, 2024

Moore, Katie, "Torturous: Lawyer questions Missouri's lethal injections protocol ahead of April Execution," Kansas City Star, February 13, 2024.

Moore, Katie, "Why Missouri witnesses could only see part of the process when Missouri executed Brian Dorsey," Kansas City Star, April 10, 2024.

Moore, Katie, "With Missouri man in execution chamber, spiritual advisor tried to show 'he was loved,'" Kansas City Star. April 11, 2024

Ortiz, Jorge L. & Sarah AI-Ashani, "Missouri Executes Brian Dorsey despite objections by dozens of correctional officers," USA TODAY April 9, 2024.

"Phenobarbital" St. Louis Public Radio, August 18, 2017

Pojman, Karen, Communications Director, Missouri Department of Corrections, Apr. 9, 2024.

Romero, Dennis. "Missouri to execute the man who murdered his cousin and her husband, governor says," NBC News, April 8, 2024.

Salter, Jim, "Condemned I could face surgery without anesthesia if the good vein is elusive, lawyers say," AP News, Associated Press News April 5, 2006.

Salter, Jim, "Missouri man executed for killing his cousin and her husband in 2006." AP News, Associated Press News, April 9, 2024.

Sanders, Matthew, " Man sentenced to die for killing his cousin in Callaway County seeks to halt execution." KMITZ April 7, 2006.

Schulberg, Jessia, "His lawyers advised him to plead guilty in exchange for nothing, now he's facing execution," Huff Post, March 19, 2024.

Shiflet, Kathy, Jonathon, Deputy Communication Director and Press Secretary at the office of Missouri Governor, announcement, April 8, 2024.

Smelser, Kathy, "Who Has Faced Execution Under Missouri Gov Mike Parson?" WDAF TV April 7, 2006.

Smith, Mitch & Ernesto Londono, "He's on death row, prison workers say he should be spared," New York Times, April 4, 2024.

Statement of Probable Cause, Callaway County Sheriff's Department Dec. 26, 2006

Unpublished Memorandum: Brian Dorsey v. Vandergriff, John Matthew Fabian, PSY.D J.D. APP Dec. 18, 2023.

Winters, Chris, Missouri State Highway Patrol Officer, interview with the victim's mother, Dec. 23, 2006.

BY ORGANIZATION

Death Penalty Information Center
Eastern Receptions and Correctional Center
Missouri Department of Corrections
Missouri Probation and Parole Board
The Missouri State Public Defender
Potosi Correctional Center
Rainbow House, Children's Emergency Shelter/Regional Child Advocacy Center

MEDIA

Associated Press News
The Atlanta Constitution
BBC News International
CNN
Columbia Daily Tribune
Huff Post
The Kansas City Star
KTVI St. Louis
The National Catholic Reporter

NBC News
The New York Times
The Riverfront Times
St Louis Public Radio
The Topeka Daily Capitol
USA Today
U.S. News
The Washington Post
WDAF TV

EMERGENCY RESPONSE TEAMS

Callaway County Sheriff's Office
Eastern Reception Diagnostic and Correction Center
Missouri State Highway Patrol Violent Crimes Support Unit

COURTS
The 13th Judicial Circuit Court, Callaway County, Missouri
Boone County Circuit Court
Supreme Court of Missouri
United States Court of Appeals
United States Supreme Court

www.ingramcontent.com/pod-product-compliance
Lightning Source LLC
Chambersburg PA
CBHW060253030426
42335CB00014B/1680